The WORLD
Far Away

and other Poems

The WORLD Far Away

and other Poems

The Backstreet

Peter Ndiwa

authorHOUSE®

AuthorHouse™ UK Ltd.
1663 Liberty Drive
Bloomington, IN 47403 USA
www.authorhouse.co.uk
Phone: 0800.197.4150

Published by AuthorHouse 05/29/2014

ISBN: 978-1-4969-8073-1 (sc)
ISBN: 978-1-4969-8074-8 (hc)
ISBN: 978-1-4969-8098-4 (e)

For Ustadh Chriches Kiplagat

Acknowledgements

I would like to acknowledge the following for their indispensable help that shaped the final form of this book:

Jacob D'sraeli: Thank you for your great advice and first hand editing of this book.

Lennox Opiyo: Your help is beyond description. Thank you.

Sheila Ayabei: I greatly appreciate your advice and encouragement.

Joseph Kimtai: Thank you for your indispensable encouragement.

Table of Contents

A fallen Dictator

Dislocated from the rank,

To the common ground of all,

His eyes behold mundane world,

A world never seen before

In the grandeur granted by forced incumbency.

A sniff-

Smell the fermented blood,

Unclaimed, for who will foot the bill

Of a casket and burial

When there is running, starvation, homelessness

All over the state?

The eloquence you had of bettering the state

Dwelled in the soar of rungs

Who cared about your pragmatics-

How you were lowering food prices

And maintaining security

In a rebel torn country

Tearing already bleeding nation

Where every food, cloth and machinery is tribal?

Sniff you fallen king,

We too have smelled for long

The scum of the earth

Restless like we've been-

Of empty protests stamped under foot

Empty speech, vacuity
Speak king, rant to the new king
For ousting you
And now worsening your errors.

Paths fore-chosen for me

In the disconcerting parliament pomP
The usual house regaliA
Infusing unfelt roT
in the defensive coutH
To settle the deliberationS

It is their wonted stufF
The quest to keep the halO
The side remaining the gunneR
Soliciting power for the next house

The chosen path a future reliC
To quell the masses wratH
That goes beyond the fake senatorial halO
Hiding the loot siphoned from public tillS
Channeled to leisure and private usE
Leaving the overtaxed masses forloN

Mine is a hollow cry as if to the deaF
The public move in a dead rodeO
Chasing unavailing justice to the letteR

Smart men denying their common hoodluM
They shamelessly return to solicit for my votE

Unplugged

Detached,
Plucked off
A long deep void-
Yet at no distance at all.

Close, yet so far;
Dead silent, yet so loud-
A cacophony, mad frenzy,
A beat-less heart yet palpitating
Beat-less time yet musical.

Silent, sea deep
immobile, yet moving,
Unsaid sentiments, yet existing
Like said.

Eyes closed, yet seeing,
Too much to say, yet no words,
What a holy spell,
Confident fear,
A lively dying heart.

Understand me love,
Form the words,
Abstract yet concrete
Love, give them life,
And know that I want you.

The unwritten poems

After the cold metallic demise of the Don
I listlessly tossed, apprehensive in the dark till dawn
When I converged to tell of this tale of a dirge
With black ink, quilt and a modern parch.
My mind whirled as I toyed with the quilt
I then saw the bullet carriers with no guilt
Like doctors, on remains carrying out autopsy;
Before the undertaker takes it without courtesy.
I thought of the tale tellers, society's eyes,
Manacled and gagged for truthfully using quilts
In my mind I saw the freedom priests
Who had amounted to mounds of ashes and pulps.
Dawn was breaking, I feared the trails
The trails that gagged, a mountain of unwritten poems.

Public emotion

That appointment they said
Would disturb public emotion
If it wasn't subtly done
With a thin disguise of tribal interests.
It backfired;
When a witty analyst
Pointed out this
To the rest of us.
You can now see that emotion
Tossed back and forth
In discussions-
On church pulpits,
Behind creaking desks
Inside public offices,
All over public squares
By hordes of unemployed youths and vagabonds-
Over breakfast shows:
A public debate.
Everyone is out
trying to unlock the deadlock
But the keys . . . cast with metals
heavily laced with tribal interests
Supplementing the half-baked credentials.

A Day of Work: Working Nation

See that child with a wet nose
Feebly running to school
Engulfed in the biting morning cold.
The torn bag of books swings by the side
The bare soles slap the cold ground.
Its teacher emerges from the tiny dilapidated room
Sandwiched between a mass of other hovels.
The pedal-less faithful bike rolls along
Its thread-less tires leaving no marks behind.
At the end of the filthy corridor
Its proud owner in a clean pair of shirt
Mounts it, the trouser carefully tucked inside socks
To avoid the greasy chain that whines along.

The road is littered with bodies
Emerging from the silent villages;
Others submerging into the same villages
Workers headed to the same villages
There where the life of the day lies.
The corroded throat of the tout has another long day
Set to shout people to work
The mason walks a long muscles fletching
The gloomy day watchman saunters on
A long day of waiting waiting for him.

The posh car noisily zooms on
A businessman going to take stocks
And there in a far countryside
The lonely train staggers a long
Picking desperate souls going to look for work
Its rusty roof packs with bodies gradually
Bodies that start dodging electric poles and thorny branches
Bodies headed to unsure destinies to work

Feet shuffle on the passages
Weary bodies trudging on
Cold silence hung inside big offices
A herdsman stands with his stick, a faithful companion
Back and forth movements sound, a working nation.

Public cleansing

Behind the black and white screen
He went on and on
Building himself an image of honesty and integrity
Subliming the mar that touched him
When he touched the public coffers.
A cleansing process devoid of confession
Ridding the bad image to nothingness
A wordy diffusion to the thin air.

Wasn't it said that the coffers and tills
Were all emptied in his private pockets?
Wasn't it ably told that the project
Was hugely inflated to a white-elephant?
Wasn't it reliably whispered;
"That man killed his way to the throne.
Women and children were set ablaze . . ."

His tongue went on
the bleary image on the screen refuted
Aptly painting a holy image with strokes of words
It subtly moved round the mound
Of lately unveiled incriminating evidence
Grim and bloody

Exorcising the demonized self
Citing the occasional good doing
Inflating it like a highly elastic balloon
To overshadow the bedeviled him.

This was grossly different
Farfetched from the report we read
Covering a couple of pages of the newspaper
Grotesquely taken too far
From what he said in the vernacular radio
Wickedly he went on cleansing the image

Untimely Death?

Who was ever invited by death
To a round-table dinner?
Where they sat and lengthily discussed
The length of life on earth
Swigging glasses of juice of life
And finally putting it to paper
With the pen of mortality
Exactly when the contract will expire
When life will ooze out
Like air escaping out of a punctured tire.

Human-beings are artifacts
Molded by the master artist.
The master artist merely watches
The made artifacts on the table
Scheming in the mind
What to polish and demolish,
All at will.
Artifacts are mute
Never protesting with the master
Whose omnipotence matches not
The mustard feeling of the artifact

We say why then
That the death of a person is untimely?
We are all mere breaths
Standing at the master's mercy
Dying infants are artifacts
Destroyed there on the wheel
In early stages of development
Oldies are well seasoned artifacts
Given more time in the kiln;
The life lived on earth.

House of precious stones

Theirs was a house
Bearing small reflections of heaven;
What of the imported furniture
Specifically ordered from abroad?
Walls were decorated
With the precious stones,
Emerald, jasper, chrysolite ornamented the walls
Almost touching the ceiling from Middle East
The smell of riches thickly hung in the air.

Exotic flowers scented the room
Editions of foreign magazines
Littered the aesthetically crafted tables.
Magazines that updated on health;
Keeping world politics fresh,
Speaking on style and art at home
Personal growth, career, relationships . . .
Everything, from world perspective

The souvenirs that scattered all about
Confirmed the numerous trips already made
To worthy local places and all over the world
Amethysts, topaz, carnelian artifacts

Testified of connection to art
Sapphire, chalcedony, beryl all the way to the loo
The whole sleepy village could be fed
For several years if the house was sold.

But . . . how could it be explained
The house now hung on a thread?
The wonderful couple divorcing, bisecting to two
For they could not agree
On the next holiday destination
Just to mark
The third wedding anniversary
Come the next month.

Genesis to revolution

A solid and dry flow
Flowing from low echelons
Rising to the high cadres.

Oppressed souls,
Burdened by obscure government policies
Slowly they get worn out
Bruised by unfair tax systems,
Lower souls getting rugged
Gradually they become strong.
In tiredness they gather strength
Hunger giving them life.
Muscles get build
Emaciation and deprivation
Born of high food prices
Depositing extra layers on them
Economic discrimination cements it all.

In joblessness youths have a lot of work
In insecurity souls fear nothing anymore
They awake, eyes wide open
Ears become wide shut
Never hearing the routine official threats

Blabbed all over the media
With no weapons at hand souls rise
Dry mouths overfed with hunger
Uttering facts, facts, facts
Facts too strong for governance theories to accommodate
Utterances that keep scholarly minds wondering
Why haven't we thought of this?

At that time sophisticated weapons fail,
They can't fight
Hunger,
Tiredness,
Anger,
A genesis to revolution.

Village Beauty unsurpassed

The sun taking a rest for the night
After a long journey of the day,
Mothers scowl at young boys
Slow at leading calves
To the cows being milked.
Men watch from a far
Leisurely starting the bonfires
To warm themselves after the long day
Their duty now finished,
The herd handed to mothers and the children
Now home from far schools.

Lazy mothers form a bee line
Mingling with the school children jamming the village well
Drawing water in preparation for the next school day
The chatter and banter echoe around the well
A bird chants sadly to its young ones
Hastily calling them home
Before the sun covers itself properly.
Night-insects' songs fill the air
Encouraged by the cooling night

Far at the village road
A lone old-man silently cycles home
The old bike squinting in the dark
Having tumbled all the way from the distant town
Where it delivered a fresh produce
To the son working in town.
A dog howls in the distance
Little flames flint in the darkness
Banana leaves rustle in the gentle wind
A drunkard finding his way home shouts
Silence gradually engulf the village
Fickle flames silently die off
The moon gently edges its way
Shining to souls dead a sleep
Wow! What other beauty is there other than this!

Portrait Dad

Safely placed away above our reach
Imposingly staring at our innocence
From the imported Italian cupboard.

His stare always followed every little move
Chilling my innocent straying hands
"He's seeing me . . ." I would halt
Warily hurrying out of the room
His eyes followed my receding body.

Occasionally he would come
From overseas or far off place
I would be kept to pace
Updating my school progress
Checking assignments and the little projects
Then He would pamper with gifts
Before disappearing the next dawn
To come back late night putting the lights on
A silhouette moving around the house
Then he would disappear again for weeks
Leaving the pompous portrait staring
Announcing the absence rather than presence.

Hope for the road

Every day I walk on this gullied road
I pity that it won't be repaired soon
And there aren't any more people willing
To salvage it from the deep running gullies.
The wind furiously blow away the soil,
The animals thin it day by day
With their huge sharp hooves that dent it.

The village women narrow it
Digging its sides for soil to paste their houses
Leaving the pits that make it crumble on the ends.
Occasional cars depress it with their big tires
Throwing the soil away in rain season skidding
disturbing it to give away its soil during the dry season.
Like a neglected man with a plaguing illness
The road suffers the depression of neglect by repairers.

But I now see hope of survival for this road
A fresh development that will mock the repairers,
The workers unwilling to repair the road
For the gullies are filling up day by day
Feeding on the floods' left over as it runs down.
The twigs and small stones are capturing soil
Patiently growing into huge mounds
That will gradually fill the gullies until they are no more.

Volition of the mad

Their fashion know no design
It neither runs out of fashion.
They are unique and in alien world,
Who understands their talk?
They are with that mindset
That no one else would have wanted
If it were for their own will.
Unknown dream they have in the
comfort of where they spend the night.
No one would like to carry what they carry
Their hairstyle costs them nothing
They know no volition yet they are sane
Then the un-courted volition pulls them back.

Killed Queuing for bread

Abandoned food shops
Vacant stalls and markets
Nay, ruined and rubbled.
Thinned population and
Thin malnourished survivors.
Here and there bakers still baked
Waiting for their end, baking for life.
Stripped menus and ingredients
Who cared for whole meals anyway?
Up the dull sky jets zoomed
Down the bakery queues spiraled
Weaving round rubble
Sweaty hands clutching bank notes
Waiting for their turn
If just they will be lucky.
Jets and artilleries
Civilian and cutlery
Hungry and angry
Jets jet their eggs
And down go hungry civilians
Bloodied and dead
Maimed wounded and killed

Pressed in new rubble and oppressed
Smelling blood and bread
Pierced with hunger and shrapnel
Knelled in a revolution
Leveled with rebels and rubble
Cornered and gunned
Gutted to the gutter
Killed queuing for bread . . .

Measurement

Floods collected in the plains
Killing people and destroying property
It destroyed homes leaving the bereft fraught
It killed leaving no corpses for burial;
It was measured in terms of national income lost.

The building collapsed in the city
Burying the inhabitants and the pedestrians
It's rubble spread all over the place
Collecting in heaps magnified by the corpses;
It was measured in terms of traffic jam it caused.

People who were killed by stray bullets
When crime was being averted-
Their corpses had no much claims
they were the sacrifice paid
In the government war against crime;
It was measured in terms of bullets wasted.

When water became a rare commodity,
taps going dry like bones
People stayed for days on end
Struggling with what was left in their systems.
It was measured as man's ability to endure.

Measurement:
The measuring rods rusted and broke,
The knobs grew stationary and rigid
The scales faded and are invisible,
Knowledge of measurement is suddenly scarce.

Black Africa's Half Life

In the heat of Africa
The scholarly rending came;
Calculating the half life
Of an element decomposing . . .
There was decomposition going on already
Slaves going across the ocean
Healthy, well vetted lot
Left behind to procreate?
Weaklings, sick-lings, the seedling
Giving birth to a generation
With half life-
Then came the second slavery
At the very backyard
Enslaving the half-life's generation
Scrambled, partitioned, segregated,
Enslaved there at home
Gagged, oppressed, exploited
Crushed, anointed with half-life . . .
Ages later in post colonial era
New errors were born
Errors of dictators and rebelling
Quashing things to under half-life
Shooting, mutilating, slaughtering,

Raping and plundering
Enslaving in dingy caves
Signing in young boys and girls
Placing them at the warfront
A forgotten lot with half half-life
Tasked with manning explosives
Young hands smeared with blood
Baptized with thirst for murder
Opiated to slaughter laughingly
Oozing out a starved half-life
A half-life surviving on hunger
Jailed in poverty and pain
Spoiled by every new oil and gold mines
Reaping blood from diamond
Left at the mercy of angry gods of gold
Caught between governments quickly changing hands
Strangled in economies struggling in deep pits
Famished and overtaxed
Paying through bleeding noses
Beings with feet hanging in graves
The black Africa's half-life.

Civilized

They know I am civilized
I know I am not. But sometimes
I think I am civilized.
I am not really learned
I am just literate and business minded.
Long trips have I made
In the name of business.
I know much of Africa, by trips.
I have seen much of Asia businesswise.
I have accidental experience
of the occidental and even Asian
and African cultural events.
But I was speculating, counting profits
And gains and sales while they lasted.
They know I am civilized
While I am not sure thinking I am.
I have amassed wealth and dress
to match and live to match.
My imported gadgets talk for me.
My foreign wife reminds them.
My overseas suits and cars and stories—
They know I am civilized but
Am I civilized?
I know I am but I think I am not.

When I rise

I have been down
For what seems too long
Kissing the earth in repentance
Donning it with supplication.

I still hear those voices
Children crying in a pit
Their voices muffled by the weeds.
They cry though they are dead
shadows of a war they never understood.

Voices of people in the run,
Come clear and fade away,
Women screaming from pain
Chocking is much louder now.

Bullets fill the air,
Landing on unaware targets,
Targets running to mistakenly shelter under bazookas,
voices of dropping tins fill the air.

I will bow much lower
Burry my face in the earth

I won't tire though I suffocate
I will wait, supplicate, repent . . .

My ears pain from strange sounds
The detonations disturb the air
Strange gases pierce my skin
It is now much refined than before

One day I will rise,
And find no one in sight
The air will all be still and dead silent
I will find no war in sight.

My eyes will see far and across
The plains will all be green
The sky will be free of strange smoke
The air will all be scented with peace.

I will rise and walk,
Explore the earth with no worry,
I will play with lively children
I will chat with everyone in sight.

We walked a mile

We leisurely walked
a single mile chatting
Who saw that man lying on a carton
Swatting flies from his wounds on the roadside?

We walked on
Past the quarry on the way,
Who saw that toothless old woman
Feebly hitting the rocks with a mallet?

We walked on past the shanties,
Smoke pouring out of them
Who saw those inside them
Busy chewing and swallowing their saliva?

Along the streets we looked ahead
Who saw those chasing a malnourished man around?
Many people hitting a feeble man
They said he wanted to steal

We walked laughing and despairing
But only for a little while-
We will keep on walking
Who will remember anything they see?

A snatched day

The comedian rehearsed
Polishing his anecdote
Till he could reflect himself in it
Seeing his stature elevated.
His was a special function:
To revive the crowd when it was dying
Falling back to inattentiveness

He mounted the dais proudly
And dawdled to his anecdote
Coloring it to perfect distortion.
The crowd went gloomy and gloomy
A wave of restlessness spreading across it.
When he left, he went a small man
So tiny that no one wanted to look at him

Then came the fledgling orator
Who commented that the crowd refused to laugh . . .
He unlocked all the gales of laughter
That went on roaring like an ocean
Till he waved them to a suppressed silence

The whispering bottle

The bottle bends down
And tells something to the glass
The glass froths with laughter
Revealing its white teeth
The worried old man under the tree
Believes this is modern technology
That miraculously solves problems
He sends the glass' laughter
Whirling down his system.
The laughter walks on stairs
and finally diffuse to the whole of him
He sleeps with no worries
He wakes up the following day
To lull his worries with the whispering bottle . . .

The story of ten young virgins

A story is told
of ten young virgins
Who climbed a tall tree
Hanging with many bee hives
The bees buzzed in the hives
Flying in and out of them.
Below the tree stood many young men
Watching them up the tree
Among the bees that had now
Learnt to treat them like fellow bees.

You take my future

You've entered my mind tonight,
Stealthy finding your way
Like a person silently groping in the dark.
Suddenly you are in my mind
Expelling sleep from my eyes

You are radiant in the mind's eye
As if stood on a bright light,
The eye watching from the dark;
You glow with beauty
Making my heart throb

The past smile presently revives
Like a radioactive element
It pierces my flesh into the heart
Making it restless and relentless
Throbbing faster and faster

Your stature is graceful
The contours tempt me to pursue them
See what wonders lie behind them
Am now breathless and take you to the future
Even though all is of the past

To a departed friend

You have now departed from us
at a time we didn't anticipate
You've to go to the earth's belly-
though you've died, you live.

I will watch the grave you will rest in
The loneliness there in is tragic.
Your red cushioned casket of honour
Lowered to the bottom of the grave
A beginning of distance between us

I will watch in anguish the red mound grow
It shields you from me
The dusty earth rises and sets on me
Mingling with tears on my cheeks
Kneading the clay I recreate you with

The mound grows high and high
Firmly wielding a barrier between us
But I know you live within me
And grow bigger and bigger
Like the mound rising.

Tearless burial

Who could shed a tear
For an unknown body?
The departure took place
in the strangers' multitude
A bloodless death, choking and charring.
We knew not the scars you had;
Your body is in no definite shape
We just say it is you
One blood with us
You will go with a dented stature
We carry out the last rite
With dry eyeballs, a tearless burial
You leave us with restless souls.
Our hearts weep for you
Though we shed no tear
In uncertainty, for the rest of our lives,
Our hearts will weep for you.

Why did you wait?

Why did you wait
Until when I had unleashed all
All of my very being
Expending all my strength
Carrying you to the great heights
Before saying you loved me not?

Why did you wait-
Until I had gone to my special pouch
And removed all my cherished arrows
To shoot unworthy hunt for you
Using my cherished arrows-
It is like a hunter wasting his arrows
On a sick hyena.

Why did you wait
Till I had opened most of my heart
And exposed the little secrets there
Sharing the most intricate me
Letting you to my very soul
Then you leave me there like a husk of nut?

Why did you wait
Why-
Till I had soared so high
Before letting me off
To fall through the empty space
Didn't you know that it hurts-
To fall from such a great height
To the empty abyss of loneliness I had left-
Oh, why did you wait
You could have told me a long time ago.
Why did you wait?

Secret mistakes

You see this is what I mean;
The honey I saw in you fermented-
I blame myself honey
I lacked that foresight.
Dear, it is all a mistake,
A secret mistake I made.
You turned so fast,
Into a bottle of vinegar.
You have become a bottle of powdered pepper,
Lashing all your bitterness on me.
My pockets are never full,
But I have tried:
Availed a chunk for the table
But . . . you make me see
Mistakes; secret mistakes.
It could have been my loneliness,
the yearning within me.
It could have been the gaping hole within,
Crying out for a companion
But I now see a secret mistake,
A mistake in tying a chord with you.

Tear and wear without repair

A foul sound is heard from the industry
A machine misdirected by the elect operator
It is noisily tearing and wearing away,
emitting foul smelling gas from the bad grinding.
The hugely priced ball-bearings falter on,
Crushing and heating the whole machine.
The input yet to be ground gets sooty
The foul gas rising over them
Soon it will be bursting into flames.

The owner stands a side helplessly watching
A dark silhouette in the rising smoke
Tears slowly finding their way down the cheeks
A silent cry from the depths of the heart
A heart than is now being pressed between the ball-bearings
And the deficient blood getting licked in the hot bearings
What a tear and wear without repair!
A heart getting transformed into a pulp-
That's where it will end if the machine won't be stopped.

Thus is bad politics;
It is a machine,
The ruled are owners of that machine.

Terrible weariness

Terrible weariness has landed down on earth:
Like a swarm of bees it is advancing
It sets forth consuming everything in sight.
Look at men, early in the morning
Before the sun has woken up,
They sit basking on rocks like geckos
Before long, they are dosing off.

What a terrible weariness
It is reducing everything to ashes.
Women have set down the diadem of hard-work
Instead they have worn the perishable wreath.
Look, they sit chatting the day away.
At nightfall they walk back to cold houses
Empty without the presence of their husbands.

Turn you from your rotting ways!
Stop dissipating the self away
Walk back to the true justice and accountability of self
Arise you men and walk to the dais
Claim back the waning ways
Hold high the esteem
And pursue this weariness into the abyss.

Dawning puzzle

The uncertainty and puzzle is melting down
   the unknown depths of the sea coming to view
No more wonder about the look
For all will see the ocean depths.
The water levels are fast falling
   Like a stone crashing through the air
The see animals wisely go deeper
   To keep living in the vaporizing water
All of us will soon see the ocean depths
From the mountain tops we will descent
Deep in the valleys we will walk
   Amongst the fossils of the animals.
The world will be like a vacated home
   The secrecy of the sky heights will be no more
We will boldly trot to the bear earth
   In sunless yet bright days
Into the surface of the ocean viewing the fossils.
   Arise now and take your belongings
Pack your tools and get ready for the walk
Across the puzzle of the dying ocean
Great scenery awaits us.

Denied pleasure

My time has come now
   To open wide a smile into a laughter
And inhale more air to sustain the laughter.
The face creases instead
Like a flower bud that refuses to open . . .

I feel full of words and desire to roll them off
   In a hearty chat with somebody
The tongue becomes heavy to lift
   The words refuse to align in order
How can they align any way?

It is my time to weep
   I feel my tear glands swollen
I heave to let them drain the tears
   the tears refuse to come out
The sob becomes inaudible

I miss the pleasure of laughter, the pleasure of chat,
the relieve of weeping
I won't have the pleasure under a leaking refugee camp roof
The pleasure won't manifest on an empty stomach
   Echoing gunshots from right and wrong people
Deny the pleasure that I dumbly mourn.

Emotionally disturbed car

That car that plies the roads
is emotionally disturbed.
It knows no rest. Day to day
Its engine gets overheated
loudly boiling like a potful of cassavas.
It is badly disturbed that car,
It knows no myriad profits
yet wants to run along the big ones.
It gets disturbed on its journeys
Paying for toll where there is no toll station
Paying for protection where there is no insecurity
It pays for mistakes in its old body
And falters down the road
Its emotions rising and falling.

Dowry-less marriage

We agreed on our own volition
to offer our daughter for marriage
to the bride of her own heart.

We've sat and waited
for the dowry as is our custom
The bride has grown blind
taking it for granted
His time for paying dowry
has unusually stretched
Our hope has been crushed
into powder that wastes away

we sit and weep
in grief and bitterness;
Of what use is an old daughter to us?

The witch

The witch was seen
Dancing and yelling among the mourners
They were mourning their beloved
Their eyes sunk with weeping.
He flaunted around with silly humour
Shouting as if nothing had been lost
Who else could be the witch?

He rummaged over the places
Looking for something to eat
See those culinary interests;
When the whole village is mourning
Grief raining on the souls
He rouses all his cravings for food
Substantiating it with silly talk.

Death of a warrior

Mourning voices disturb the evening peace
The demise of a warrior,
Who will fight for us?
Many wars you have fought
None left you scathed.
Your fame went beyond the ridge;
Now what has killed you?
You depart by mistake
Falling on your own spear.

You well knew how to hold your shield
Finding your way among the enemies
Slaying them till the last one
Your glory burned brighter and brighter—
What a guttery way you have died!
Mysterious, your own spear
Couldn't you see your own spear
Badly placed around you?
We will shed tears with estrangement

Spoiled age

They themselves
    Fired the cannons
That spoiled the road

They were far back then
    They now need the road

They hold their breath
    As they stealthily find their way
Round the abysses

What a walk;
What an age!
They live by spoiling

The prophesied days

Soldiers cling to the barrels of their guns
  Feebly leaning on them like walking sticks
The dreaded war sound has been heard
Far at the horizon it still is
But it is deafening and paralyzing
Making them sick at heart

They groan and lament at their fate
Their necks stiff in a bow of terror.
All the kingdoms have risen against them
Refusing the tribute they offered to pay them
The soldiers weep drowning their duns with tears
Lamenting the destruction about to come on them

The prophesied days are now here at hand
Pruning forks beaten into spears
No tribute nor treaty will ever avert the prophesy
The soldiers cry like infants with faint hearts
Women and children wail in misery
The war sound is getting thunderous and deafening

Last night

Last night I was in another world
My spirit rode the wind
The future met the past
My heart pounded away
The eyes didn't like bright light
But the pitch darkness
Where my spirit softened
and was tender

What confidence was there in me!
Fearlessness and conviction-
I could walk the whole earth
On my own in darkness
I couldn't fear any storm
Living had been dulled
Its tautness slackened;
In the pitch darkness.

Sleep wasn't of any use
My mind went blank yet thinking
Unsolicited smile
danced on my lips.
The whistling wind
caressed my spirit
My soul got rest
And fused with the spirit of the wind.

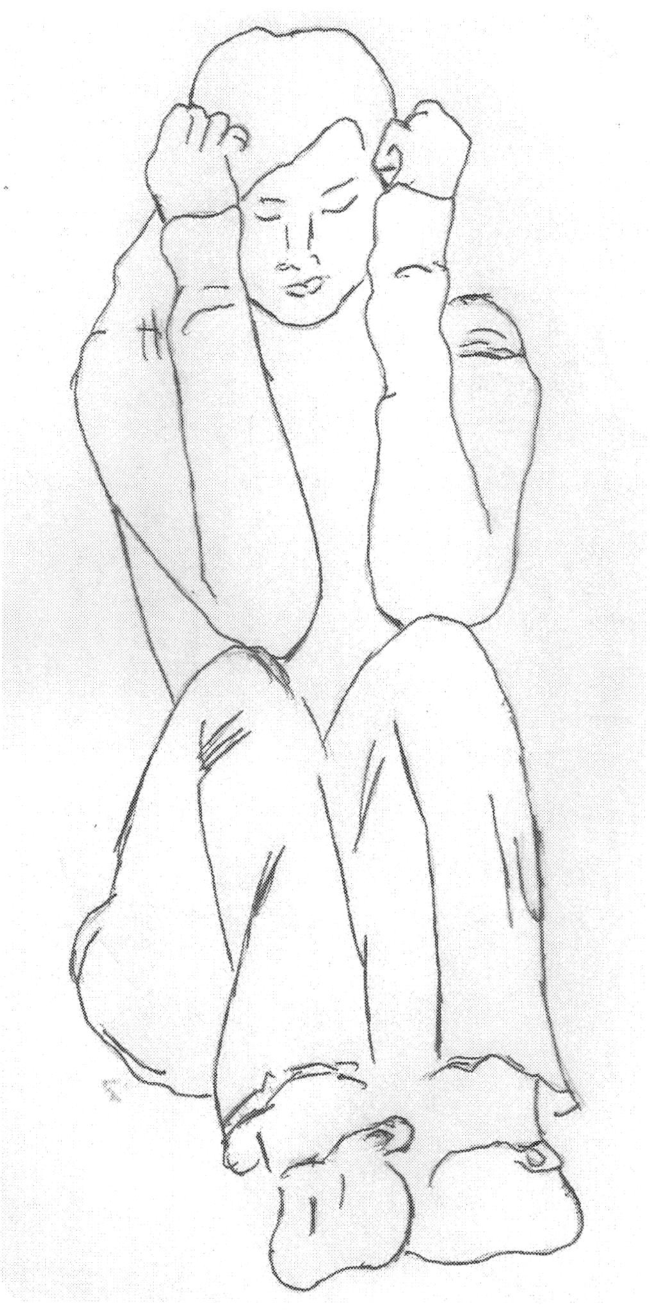

Death of a poet

Never has the death of a poet been told
With so much tears flowing
In streams down the cheek
Who saw the death coming?
Who saw the arrow sail the air
Aiming for the poet's tender heart?
What a death-
None will ever know the poets secrets

He is remains
Mysterious that the life on earth
Paid him no homage.
Affection and nostalgia still remain
Even as the journey to the soil begin
Unsolved mysteries stay behind
Strange secrets the poet carried
Making the mourners weep in a splurge

Intellectual property in matrimonial property Law

Upon shredding of the marriage
When it can no longer hold
and the percentages of gain
and not emotional pain
distributed;
Shouldn't it be logical too
that intellectual property be protected?

The aesthetic arrangement of furniture
splendid interior decoration ideas
curtain techniques and mural hangings
exterior gardening and flower pot techniques
shouldn't the intellect at that be protected too
so that the rightful soul remains with the rights
of such wits and efforts?

And the fresh bed time jokes
and fine love notes exchanged
should also feature somewhere.

The journey to the absent sea– When water first flowed

It was cumbersome on that morning
The earth wept incessantly
Its tears gathered in gigantic globules
That flowed on the surface of the earth
Seeking their destiny—the absent sea

It was a faltering filled with determination
To find a path on the rugged surface.
Getting obstructed by the steep hills
Water whirled and rushed down
Falling through the air
To another lower earth

A rock provided an easy flow
But not with its particles.
Many days later water leisurely walked in the plains
Trudging to the unknown
What a struggle this was?

The sun is a robber
From a far it sent its rays to the surface
Freely stealing the waters' tired sons and daughters

In bitterness their mothers remained behind
Forming the salty lakes
The remaining got determined
Forging on in determination
It was late in the evening
Some months later
When worn-out rivers met and merged
Collecting and mingling in tiredness
They refused to flow anymore
Deciding to joyously dance in wavy movements
They called themselves a sea
And smiled in blue.

Sudden Death

What manner of death this is
That crept in stealthily
Without even a single knock
And stole him away
Without even a single last breath?

He majestically walked
Loudly and jovially laughed
Broadly talked of the future
With so much hope and health
Then all of a sudden was without a heartbeat.

He is like a chopped off branch
Withering on the earth surface
A transformation to being a soil particle
But what manner of death this is-
That cuts a person at his summit?

A death that comes with no ailment
Nor a bullet cutting through a tender heart
The death walks with a person
Clinging to his garments wherever he goes
Then like a falling machete smitten him.

Modern coronation

Samuel trudged on wearily
  With a mourning heart
And a horn full of anointing oil
  To Jesse's home to anoint a chosen king
Among Jesse's sons

A biased beginning he had
  Looking at the outward appearance
Neglecting David looking after sheep in the bush.
Anointing oil refused to flow
  Until he was brought in and anointed, Lords chosen.

What would have happened in modern days?
The horn would have been broken
And the anointing oil lifted on dirty fingers
And scarcely applied on a biased one
And ululations forced for the 'chosen king'.

The distant song

My ears caught a distant song
Drifting on in obscurity
Infecting me with a desire to join it.

In a haze I was in vault
Distorted images of singers drifted by
Distant beats sounded in diminuendo and crescendo
Where were the singer's standing?

My mind caught the beat
Fast complex and sad
It beat my logic at first
Before I finally caught

It caught me strongly
I rose from the pew
Hazy images flying by
I strained my vocal and joined the song.

I was shouting and clapping
Knocking my fists for effect
Swinging limply to the obscure beat
Before I was drained of my energy

I woke up on the floor
Drowned in water that revived me
They asked me what the matter was
I muttered and went to sleep.

Half a man.

I was half asleep and half awake
My heart pound in half a beat
I dreamt a blurred dream
Suffocated and half-dead
I wept tears flowing down one eye
I listened to voices in on ear
Strange voices from between heaven and earth

I was chased down a steep hill
I ran on single leg
Supporting myself with my arm
I broke into two, dissected vertically
What haziness this is
I breathe using my one nostril
I live, half a life.

Thinking the hard way: Measurement

We have no sense of measurement,
we measure in vain or better, one way.
The old scorched memory knows not
the other sense of measurement
It pretends by reflecting in the old way.

In what units is that measuring rod?
You hold it on the crooked surface
And peer at its faded calibrations
Ignoring the dented and weathered ends
Approving its accuracy with a subtle nod.

You brought the rope you used
To estimate the recent measures.
You stretched it on the ragged opening,
then followed it with your old measuring rod
And recorded the measurement on a scrap of paper.

We will now sit restlessly
Waiting for your conversions
Appropriating the measurement on the old table
The truncating it and rounding it off
Then finally announce your esteemed findings.

The Rich Fool

The rich man paced importantly
With calculated steps
Trotting the rich ground of his farm
That had brought forth plentifully.

His thoughts raced
In unnatural competition with his sight
As he summed up his own worth
Reflected in the shiny grains.
What shall I do with all these?

The spirit of contingency awakened in him
The mind's eye peering deep into the future
The ambition overtook him:
"I will pull down my barns and built
Bigger ones . . . . ! He concluded.

He summoned all unsatisfied appetites
Drawing deep from the past.
Appetites for drink and food came live,
His soul pleasantly relaxed.

From his big heaven,

God watched patiently

The fool drawing his mighty plans.

With a wry smile on his face

God collected the value of his life

Summing it in his book of life

It came to nothing

It couldn't be distinguished from poverty.

Finally looking away to more serious matters

God concluded;

"I just have to harvest, you,

Into my barns . . . later this night."

Simon Peter on The Shore

Vainly casting the net
Into the empty black waters.
Lonely in the cold chilly night.
Dark uncertain thoughts danced in his foggy mind.
Restlessly he paddled, disturbing the waters;
Nothing happened. The fish proudly stared
And swam away from his ominous net.
He dismally swallowed and wearily stared
into the darkness. Nothing stirred;
Only the silent wave of the dark waters
gently slapped against the sides of the old boat.
The night wore on. The fish swam away
To spend the night in deep waters
Away from Simon Peter's deadly paraphernalia.
The lure proved futile, testing his patience.
Nothing happened. The sun woke up and found him there,
Finally he paddled to the shore to wash the nets.
The sandy shore was cold, his thoughts frozen.
Then Christ came, fishing in the hopeless population
Gently he asked him, "Can I use your boat?
He had no objection. The day slowly matured.
Then he found himself a fisher of men.
With a patient smile he had been caught;
In Christ's big net, with the help of his boat . . .

The red leaf in the lake

I clung to the paddle
And shoved the waters
Whirling ominously
Refusing to obey my paddling

The current opposed me
I knew I would capsize
Till the red leaf came tossing
And floated boldly behind

A strange taste formed in my mouth-
I wondered how far it had come
How had it survived?
I feared the storm no more.

Vanity

I have never been ambitious.
Never, Not on earth;
Or if I have ever been,
Then it was in futility.

I look through a dilated eye
And see her two faces,
Overlapping over one another,
These, vague images.

My heart has never throbbed,
My breath has never left me,
No spasm has ever hit me.
Not when I have no feelings.

I have no fears, only pity
I have walked the darkest night
unperturbed, no loss will I encounter
I won't run, only stare blankly.

She stretches her golden bow,
Clutching the string of uncured leather
Let her balance the arrow between her fingers,
Tiny space in her fingers, the long I have loved.
Her twin shadows aim the arrow,
They now are two jeweled arrows
I am unperturbed, I have no fears
She will miss the single trunk, me.

The return

Lights had long gone out
Crowning darkness jovially.
Night creatures were dead
Or either were veiled in sorrow.
Nothing stirred, not even the wind.

It was as black as death
Sadness had descended on earth
Swooping like an eagle
It had stretched its talons
Ensuring nothing eluded it

The crunch of feet was too loud
They locked in a battle with the earth
Betraying the perturbed heart
Magnifying every slight move ominously
I was crushing into wretchedness

The eyes misted involuntarily
Lamenting in the dark.
This was outright betrayal.
I had been mercilessly besieged
For I had gone in bright light.

Waiting on the shore

Waiting inside a vacant mausoleum
Could have more hope than here;
Waiting an un-purged sea shore
For the unpredicted arrival
Of a clumsy alien ship

He sat on the soil
Staring blankly into the deserted sea
His empty mind danced on the froth
He kept refilling his lands occasionally
Inhaling the frowsy dead air

No bird danced
There was no life
The sea was dead, No waves.
He was neither afraid nor courageous
Casting occasional glance to the distance
Surveying the horizon of the sea.

His hope was slowly dying
He kept chewing the tasteless bone
To keep the hope going.
With the countenance of a waning smile
He met his death by the shore.

Many months later

The alien clumsy ship docked.

There was no ceremony, no reception.

The skull was staring with its sockets.

The ship returned to the Dead Sea and journeyed back.

Weird night music

A body walks the skies
In the depth of the night
It raises its golden fingers
Bejeweled in sorrow
And plays melancholic music
Striking keys of an ancient piano

It is restless, that body
Slowly it walks in somnambular manner
Touching the skies' horizons
Its music and footsteps fade away
And ominously return growing louder

It is strange, unfathomable
Sometimes slapping the keys
Or slowly walking its fingers on them
Then speedily vibrating a finger on a key
Then playing a drowsy sad tune
Plucking off the keys to silence

Never

He NEVER knew her
She *never* said so
They **never** showed it

She *never* said anything
Only commented
Not on what he NEVER said

They **never** agreed
Disagreed, they NEVER
None proved that

She *never* had feelings
She **never** showed
He NEVER understood

It was puzzling
Never clear to them
They **never** said so

They NEVER meet now
They don't talk, NEVER
None of them understands, *never*

To the young ones

Children, I have walked the earth,
Not just physically
But by the mind also.
I have gone far,
My eyes surveying the emerging horizons;
The sea too has got a horizon.
You have embraced coronation,
Up from infancy;
You now have little muscles that can walk-
Watch the earth you tread young ones.
I have seen marshes along the way,
Some breed sweet smelling perfumes
And are overgrown with weeds-
Be wise and pass.
Strange birds will sing you praises
Leading you to dingy roosts to dote,
Watch the horizons children
Scan and attempt to unravel
All that you see there
Then calculate your moves
Choosing the nestled path.
Edge with a smile
To the good you have deciphered
Children, go now

Doused flame: Death of an activist

His second flash
Had no choice of a dance
In the knight attempt
That was sure to burn brighter
Unveiling the numerous governance flaws

Scarlet had to be his departure
An uncouth chop off speedily executed
The heavy metal jetting forth
Landing on the flame hastening for a revelation
In the second growing glimmer

The muddled activism wick blinded,
Doubtfully stagnating in-between
Sucking the fuel to the absent flame
Crumbling down and splashing the fuel
In a permanent abscond away from the dropping metal

The growing lantern was killed
Activists melted into shadows
Timorously hanging in worry
Debating whether to catch another flame
Or disintegrate to its quelled incipience
Meanwhile, we tread in darkness hopelessly

A wonder of image

He had no definite name
Only known through a pseudonym
That bore little shadowy semblance
To his formless existence
That sadly nobody paid homage to.

He eked a living through occasional alms
At such times gratitude was his-
But he still nudges the mind
Prodding it to form an image for him
Even if in an inept staggering sketch

He rests, in the belly of the earth,
Nobody mourned for him, only sympathized.
He was no prophet, though he lived like one
He was not insane. He had countless scruples
There is no allusion or metaphor for him

He has escaped from this world
Soaring away in a scraggy coffin
Austere, mend from rotting cheap wood
He will stagger out of minds-
Leaving behind a wonder of image

The backstreet

There is no espousal
To flee from the stench
Drifting from the gutter
The inexhaustible source

There is no respite,
Nor choice for fresh air,
Else, that equals empty stomach
That luxury of leisure won't quench

There is no choice either,
On all weather moods
Eking is a deathless manner
That forever stays in the ghetto

Hope dies with a gone life
And the living ensnare other hope
Gaping into the mound of slough
Extracting a living from it.

Abandoned

Sodden sand with footprints-
And a forgotten downpour . . .
There stood the sand ladder
Stooping on the sand heavenwards.
Indolence too pervaded the place;
The castle must be full now
Evident from the innumerable footmarks,
Left on the frail rungs.
Amazing; all humanity had ascended.
I stood at the ladder's foot
Like Jacob in the desert dreaming
Of angels descending and ascending a heavenly ladder.
I gazed at the food crumbs on the sand,
There was no cottage for me to rest.
I vigilantly tried the rung with my foot
It came crumbling to my feet-
It never landed;
Wind blew it away forming a thin sheet.
I made a skeptical move
And lumbered through it savagely
Hoping if they will crash back
They won't land on me.

I will walk now

I will rise and walk now
Away from this lonesome self,
To that comely palace I have seen
Far yet so close
Gallant, adorned with gentleness.

My eyes are now open
Her radiant heart irresistibly calling
I will journey on in patience
Borrowing on all my wisdom
And in sagacious deliberation
Settle in the land's elegance
For why will I want to go back?

A midst dark shadows I have considered it
Transfixed, immobile yet raring to go
And dwell in the benevolent land
In the halo of love and fragrance
Rising from her tamed personality

Beat-less heart is mine
Yearning for that land's union.
The wind witnesses the restlessness,
The moon advocates for me to go
And every falling night beckons me to go.

The void in us

There is that void in us
That distends with every satisfaction
That we manage to grab in won onslaughts.
It descends too in lost pursuits
Like the back move of a saw
It viciously cutting through
Demanding in vain to be sate

The fate of those men and women-
Trapped inside alehouses;
Looking through glazed glassfuls.
They are hoisted aloft the voids
And with drunken gaiety and laugh
Become alien to the voids

What trails the atonement?
The void gapes in a mammoth inflation
The ripple augments beyond the eaves
Bearing taciturn voids that silently nag;
Throbbing the spirit to voracious search
That unearths more voids within

And we live
In the taverns, and the orgies,
The hunting of dough sleeplessly;
Zealous hermits and hermitage,
And the endless epistemology
On and on the voids rage.

Conversation with King Solomon

I too king, in the depths of latter centuries
Have thought of these things and converged in vanity.
You see king, in these modern days of democracy,
They have ruled, looted and plundered:
They too like you have left with no satisfaction.
Did you loot King? Allow me to forget that first;
The women; how did you manage with them?
They still secretly exist around palaces today.
I have known no wisdom yet, only education
And I too have engulfed sorrow like you.
It dwindles my hope; toiling for the wind.
How peerless you were king;—you revered pleasure,
embraced drinking, yet contented in your work.
Abreast of times, king, we've nightmares;
No proper work. The dreaming thing-
How about that; "they come with many cares . . ."
These short ones, the political dreams, aren't they nightmares?
I too with my eyes have seen vanity!
Your officials, king, had eyes ascending in superiority;
Up the judicial ladders. Yet you saw no justice?
Vanity. I'm blind yet have seen it too.
'Cast bread upon waters; you shall find it'

A good line king; but bread is expensive,
And no water either. Vanity, king, vanity.
Meaningless! Meaningless! It's good to revere God
Behold when the earthly palaces kill soon
Heavens might give the missed rest.

Rusty golden dance

That dance; in golden space,
Handled by golden hands
Generously laced with gold-
Giving them the smooth touch.
The wriggling, like boneless worms,
Making a jig on the earth's surface
The motivation; the depriver?
The scentless fragrance of golden steam,
Rising around the arena
In sparkling royalty of gold.
Strange: dancing to beat-less dumb gold-
And what gold did catch rust
Smutting on its edges,
With the transformation of the golden steam?
The effigy does remain,
A mockery to a beat-less golden dance.

Foretold death

If I am to die on this road
Then I knew it a long time ago
When I saw the vision
of my unceremonious demise
sure to be on this road
In my numerous journeys across it

If really I am to die
Then let no one shed a tear for me
You have known it all a long
That mine is a survival, not a life
Risking my life trotting this road.

I know I have to die
A journey back to the soil
Let it be no cause of sorrow
Mine is a foretold death
Imprinted in your minds with the ink of fate.

Heart of stone

I never knew of such a heart
So emotionless as if dead
Such is the stubborn heart
That shakes hands with death
Patting it on its back
Fearing not to welcome it to its premises

What a heart that doesn't weep?
It broke down the seas of tears
And built cisterns full of holes
The heart knows no grief or joy
It has never shed a tear down its dry cheeks

Flee from such vicious heart
Take the heart of flesh
The heart ever green with emotions
Watered by eternal springs of fresh waters
Weep in sorrow and joy

The world far away

There exists that world
Self styled in its own brand of austerity
Ordered with a constellation
That sets unchanging times for it.
Those dilapidated buildings abandoned
And a wall, like the wall of the universe
Fortifying their dark pools of stagnant water
The inhabitants move about
Carrying weights back and forth
Some ride in carts
Towed by long horned bulls
faltering on a long the rutted roads.
The ancient lorry
Drives across the dark pools
Children cheer it as it splashes water
Men and women work incessantly-
Lost in trades in hope
And at the end of their world stands a vision-
A rusty ladder hanging loosely
They will climb a long it to the sky,
When hope will lower its rungs a little bit.

The fleeing

The descend that had become of us
Dark rivers murmuring their way
Down the drying valleys losing elegance
And the rhythm of gunshots and explosives echoing
The dreadful loneliness had marked the desertion

What was the fate of our cities?
The big houses abandoned
Where had the owners ended?
On the mountain tops and valleys
Drunk fighters chatted and laughed in gaiety

The lead liberal voice called
Clearly costing on the wind
Saying we had useless sorrow
The dread too had no impact
For why would we mourn the death-
For dictator who had remained for decades?

It called for our return,
To the besieged cities and dwellings
A new promise had been made
Time wheeling by testing its toll
We had to return to the city.

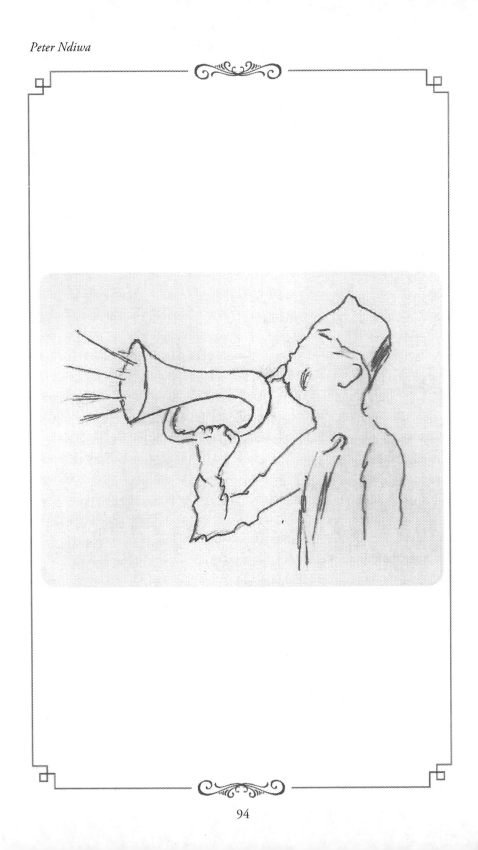

Strange Bereavement

I won't pay a damn
Who was she to him anyway?
He is so sentimental,
Catching unwarranted nostalgia
His hands sorrowfully clasped,
Holding his aged chin in reminiscence.

Did she live a single breath
Or leave mysteriously and vanished?
Who wants to think of her?
Not me. I won't pay a damn
To this strange bereavement
That shakes his voice in numerous narrations

Deep in the distant past
Does the bereavement have to keep coming
From the pages of a torn book he read
Infecting him every evening
Is it that the bright sun suns it away?
With its setting
The artistic bereavement revives
Keeping his eyes wet throughout the night
What manner of bereavement is this?
Not me, I don't want to imagine it.

The smell she left

The smell she left-
Neither scent nor odour
Neither sweet smelling nor pungent-
What is it that it has grown defiant
And refused to go away?

She never had any raisins
Nor the slightest traces of calamus
Or those high minded scents
Just some obscurity in the senses
That thickly hung with mysterious smell

The toll of the bell incessantly ring
Perturbing the mind in half remorse
Faltering in a coy reprimand
Lagging at the back of the mind
Continually keeping that smell.

The memory

I never breathed a word to her
Yet she lingers in my mind
Defying the distance and time.
I swear she never even noticed
My presence and existence around her

May be it is her air
That continually nudged my fingers
To delicately ran across them
Breathlessly looking into her eyes-
Milk-white with shinny dark pupils

It could be that smile
That she generously lashed out
To her acquaintances and close friends,
In their merry chats;
Those lips weaved sweet words

She always left me breathless,
Unaware of such nudging in me
Her lithe body swinging with every move
She now moves in my mind
Why can't she walk out
If not down to my heart?

Misplaced triumph

You sounded the royal drums
And rung the bells
Calling out for the magnificent celebration.
What is that magnanimous leap you paint
In those animated colourful songs?
Deep within the weathered souls
We sing sorrowful dirges
Accompanied by those forced tunes
Playing on your government instruments

We won't content in the scenery;
And that disturbed wildlife
That you bet counts the mileage
Metering out the economic milestones
The government strived to achieve.
It more develops naturally
Forming no mutuality with the economic strategies
Flickering with those descriptions
Embedded on the royal tunes

The songs rise to the heavens

Disillusioning weak souls in its contours

What about the economic scum that litters the surface?

You gaze at the dream beauty skillfully painted

You don't look at the debris of failure

There at your very feet

Gaze keenly, and you will see sorrow triumphing in you.

Ashes of War

Women and children:
Weaponry is not their field
Power is not their obsession
Politics not their collective interest-
What do they have to do with mine-fields?
The latest discoveries
of gold and diamond,
Crude oil crudely clawing
At their innocence

What do women
Who spend all days
Tending small gardens
Have to do with minerals?
What do children who chase after goats
Wiping wet noses
Have to do with political allying?

Rebel glowering spreads
A war of loyalists and rebels
Stepping on women and children
Men have gone to war fronts

Armature and dexterous hands
Hitting it out at the front
Capturing and losing fields
Ceasefires reviving
Mediations widening rifts
Sucking in more and more
The women and children
And the international voices harshly rasp
Sanctions and sanctions
Slapping across the faces
Of the tender vulnerable set
Women and children
Burning
Enslaved
Confined to forces camps
Dying like flies in sewers.

A raw ending

It surely can't be
That we sat in the dewy bushes
Clinging to the barrels
Courting more hope with the starry nights
That at last we will return
To the land that threatened to bury us

It could have been a dream;
Better or worse a nightmare
Every morning rising
Mended the weary souls about to break
Rejuvenating us to relentlessness
That saw our emergence from the abyss

We emerge with no ceremony
No slightest stirs at our presence
But detached nonchalant stares
As though we were yet other murderers
Just released accidentally from prison
We have become the unfortunate misfits

Who cares for us?
We salvaged riches in wrong hands
Fought the dreaded devils
Are hovels only our fitting reward
And the withering plantations to the horizons?
Was this what we fought for?

Stormy departure

When I think of that sight
Rusty blue lantern lamp burning
Casting a huge shadow on the faces
An eclipse of the soot on the cracked chimney
Everything was ghostly in the dingy room
The faces sweating in sorrowful mourning

The great chief had passed
His indelible image will forever remain
A grey hat resting on his wise head
A simple stripped tie hanging on his neck
His casual modest dressing
Punctuated by the black leather shoes

He talked with deep acumen and great prowess
Uniting locals in the expanse under the palm tree
No crowd had ever matched his before
The wind rustled softly in the warm morning air
Blowing leaves about peacefully in accord with the chief;
A permanent grief, a huge dark cloud that may not pass.

Disturbing Images

I am not talking of elderly men
Weeping in excruciating bitterness
Watching their property and relatives perish
In the instigated political upheavals
Neither am I talking of the homeless
Suffering in the harshness of weather
Rushing in through the rotten tents

I don't want to mention the meager earnings
Of the civil servants and the protests
It is not about the street hawkers battling it out
With the council foes in the chasing battles
It is not the freaky buildings burying people
That is not what I am talking about
But a terrible queer image in totality

I have seen the disturbing images
The darting eyes flickering momentarily
Up from the bill papers making grand proposals
Enriching the splendor of the achieved political dream
That left undying nightmares in its wake
Yet they still want it to pass them to glory
At the cost of masses retreating
Into in-ascendable abyss.

The doom days

Those days that were spoken of
Many millenniums ago by our fore fathers
In those years that have gone yonder
Passing behind those lone black horizons
Those days, the dreary unfathomable days
They have calmly drudged on and are now here

You can see the folks wandering about
They stare blankly at the days and match ahead
But they see nothing, only bleak images
See the dexterous hand wittily withdrawing
And meekly and despairingly resting in empty pockets
No one shakes hands with these days

The days dwell within the disillusioned folks
And the folks dwell within the dry dead days
Days dry as heated stones, with no feelings
You can see them awkwardly staring each other
As if about to rise into a cowardly fight
But it is impossible, it is all abstract war

It is now a square pity all over the land
See the old men resting weary hands on bald heads
Sitting on the bare barren ground in devastation
The women staring on in half pity
Their faces dry with uncertainty, devoid of feelings
The children and youths melted away to vanity

The supple wind lazily drifts through the land
How pitiably it fells the men and women
It blows the forlorn buildings of the towns
Forcefully closing the rotten and rusty doors
It has converted many into smart man eaters
For how else do you dream of tomorrow
With an empty stomach?

The old fragrance and jollity have left the land
Slowly vaporizing giving room to the stale air
The boulders have disentangled from the cool mountain tops
See how now they litter the surface of the earth
Who can walk any further comfortably on the paths
The days, the doom days are now here.

The reverend goose

You can revere that goose
Foolishly flapping about like an infant pigeon-
Where has it drawn that notion
That it is a modern way of flying?
Revere it for its unique capability
To be a gosling while well aged
The geese wedged to the coast
Descending unto costly gaggles
Just at the moment when there was a demand
That there be accountability on the stolen pellets
And the strangling and the bloodshed they caused
High they sore at the sight of trouble
Emanating from their errors on clarion calls
The chosen geese have all gone wild
The old geese have taught the young the tricks
They all too have come to know the art
And the game they play at heart
Tame them, let them be emissaries to the house-
Once they get to the esteemed house
And settle on the coveted seats of the house
Deep in to the comfortable cabins

Poor you who tamed the goose
For, what tamed creatures get wilder?
Revere the geese in grudges
Revere the geese for the witticism
Revere them for getting wilder when tamed!

To the wind

A howl,

Distant;

Like that of a lamenting dog;

I shout,

I mourn,

To the wind.

The black soil cling,

To my tattered bottom;

As I sit on,

Mourning, dwarfed,

Hoping my cry will clamber,

Find its way up the ranks.

With the immensity of fusty air,

Expelled from the lungs,

I sigh the lament,

Shrunk to a noise

A common place noise;

To the wind, to the wind!

Heels full of black toes,
Clothing bathed in soot,
A walk to the ranks
Loud proclamation,
No national response,
It ended in the wind.

Invisible being,
Just like wind
Shrunk, squeezed, broken
Lungs drawn of air,
Hand and feet drained
Now rise and walk!

Flap about,
Like fish out of air,
No soil to cover you,
A storm whirled in it
You too have whirled
Invisibly,
To the wind,
Silence.

A grey sunset

A cold evening,
Un-cherished, unnoticed moment;
The demise of the sun
And the demise of a son
He was here, just the other year
Unseen growth, like under thicket
The moon rises unperturbed
Mourning desperately fills the air
Morning didn't give a clue
That a son was dying

The wind rustles its endless tune;
What does it think of this demise?
See the dry faces staring ghostly-
The eyes exhausted of tears wearily retreating
Deep into the unsure sockets;
Who saw this death coming
Brutally making for this young soul?

The grave's mound draws incessant tears,
The lowering of the casket lowering souls

And the sun goes on shining
The moon rises as usual
Appearing and disappearing
Rivers flow on as if nothing happened
And the demise forever lives with us.

Happy festive season?

How can it be?

A happy new year-

A good morning;

When the last of the blood drops

Still flowing in the veins

Is being sucked every new day

With the sky rocketing food prices?

How can I be happy

When life has become compulsory slavery

Operating between the hand and mouth?

We are pulps being ground

On the grinding stone of bad economy

The wheel gyrates

Spinning with struggling lives

Till we drop dead

On the grinding floor.

Can that be happiness?

When an invisible hand

Is slowly squeezing the neck

Closing its ugly talons

On already choked lot

How can I respond to
A happy festival message?
Is it good morning or good mourning?
Happiness won't suffice
On a scale standing on a shot pivot-
Seasons are senseless
As long as there is a bane in the mind

Auditor lover

Sweet, so sweet a love
But with different sweetness:
Your sweetness and my sweetness.
Your aptitude of beauty kept me gazing
Gazing at you, but I missed guessing
Guessing at what awaited at the horizon.

Deep into your eyes I stared,
With a gentle roll you made me read love
Alas! Your stare was not a stare
But a clever audit
Of the worth in me; materially.
The depth of my love
Was your depth of my pocket,
The breadth of my love
Was your breadth of my wallet;
Yet you made me believe
It was love that was carrying us
As we journeyed to the deep future.

With your gentle words
I could see love blazing
With your sweet promises

I could see hope growing
You made a cosy world for me
But nay; it was a preparation
For the smithereens my heart was to break to
When we would come to that point
When you would finish your audit
When you would sum up the worth
of us two you secretly weighed.

Long the love lasted to me;
I should have smelled muskiness
You confused the musk with scent
That technically oozed
with your clever words.
Your lips plaited sweet words-
Nay; they were a spider's web
That broke with little weight

I should have asked:
"What makes this love last long?"
Blindly I asked;
"What will make this love break?"
You had the answer-

My trodden worth
That was far from toppling the worth
Of your other lover
You never said so:
Only let my heart drop
Smashing to smithereens
When you had wiped my worth away!

The sculptor

The sculptor skillfully worked
Reproducing the image in his mind
On the shapeless stone.
His patience underwent test
Waiting for the day the stone
Will match the image in his mind
All contours pursued to their mark
And unwanted pieces curved off.
He produced the first image
And worked shaping it accurately.
He polished it till it shone
Resembling a supernatural creation
And on putting the final touch,
The last polishing move,
The sculpture broke into pieces . . .

The woman on the Rubble

You have seen that woman
Sitting on the rubble weeping.
Her lap is drowned in tears,
Her spirit departed from her.

You have seen her,
Her face veiled in sorrow:
Hidden behind a thick piece of cloth
Mourning her children buried in the rubble.

She has searched the rubble,
She is bleeding from the unfruitful search.
Her hope has faded and worn out,
She doesn't want to see the world anymore.

She seats on the rubble weeping,
Weary with sores on the soles of her feet
She is too tired to search any inch
She now mourns waiting to join her children.

Second cremation

They have laid the urn ready for cremation
In grief and bitterness;
To pay the last tribute to the departed
Lying in the urn, mocking
For he is ash, already cremated.

When he lived in the furnace,
Sacrificing his life to exist;
The guns exploding and smoke choking
He tossed in every new wave.

He got misshaped and dented,
Every one claiming the right path
To the destiny of eternal living.

Everyone claimed a better manager,
Well placed to distribute resources.

The return wave got turbulent,
It went partly and died.

He rarely saw it. He now is ash,
Mocking from the urn,
Ready the second cremation.

Counting the dents

He could have married decades ago
But he kept counting the dents.
The first woman he met for marriage
Had a rather irritating laughter.
Then came the one with silly coyness,
He couldn't bear all these.

All was not lost, he still had
A large pool to choose from.
The next wasn't without her faults:
All was perfect and desirable
Except the scars on her feet
Could one live with them for the rest of his life?

White hair came knocking
But still one could take his time.
The next was unreasonably nagging
Demanding more praise from him.
"This will wear me out," he thought.
Another one didn't just take her time to accept.

He counted the dents to his age of degeneration.
Others had tough manly hair
Without his desired feline gait.
They came and went away like the sun
With suspicious piercing looks, taciturn women,
He kept on counting the dents.

Let the rain come down

Let the rain come down in bitter torrents
Furiously beat on my soar eyes
And mingle with my incessant tears
Wash away all the bitterness down my freckled face
So that all may not notice my tears any more.

Let the rain come down in floods
Floods that tear down my tired back
And save me the burning burden of life
That depletes and wears me away
Carrying other peoples imposed loads.

Let the rain come down in light showers
And soothe all the un-healing sores on my body
That dries then festers to torment my frail body.
Let it numb all the taut aching in my heart
That denies me peaceful hours of sleep.

Let the rain come down
In bitter torrents, in floods, in light showers
Let the rain come down in angry storms
So that if it won't sooth me, comfort me, heal me
Then let the stormy rain kill me.

Tonight the moon will rise high

Tonight the moon will rise high
Patiently edge on to its highest point
From where it will silently stare down on earth
And smile its waning mysterious smile
Motivated by the affluence and poverty
That litters the earth under its bright face.

Tonight the moon will rise high
Just for the sake of the bleeding heart.
Its rays will pour down in mystery
And land on the bleeding heart down on earth
It will form a dark shadow of pain linked to it
As the blood gathers into a large pool that spread in streams.

Tonight the moon will rise high
High enough as if fulfilling a rendezvous
With the empty stomachs that pain in ulceration
It will clearly show the desolateness of the coiled intestines
That has narrowed down as if begging for little food
Just enough to fill the space about to close in a life.

Tonight the moon will rise high
It will illuminate the fresh grave of a departed fellow
A danger to yet another important secret plan.
It will burn bright in commemoration of evidence destroyed
Send to the insatiable belly of the earth
The moon will rise high;
timidly reflect in the tears of the bereaved.

Tonight the moon will rise high
Its tears will reflect the light
That will mock the guards and masters of the secret plan.
The moon will weep itself bright in pain
An assertion to point out the justice kept under foot
The moon will faithfully burn crying for justice.

The moon will rise, O' it will
Just tonight to prove itself faithful.
It will reveal the opulence and poverty
It will reserve more light for the despondent
The poor fast speeding towards death
Tonight the moon will rise high, O' it will.

Dirty bounce: walking in the slums

It is no longer the calculated steps,
Varying the length and searching
With the eyes of your feet;
For the better place to step
And walk across the murky ground.

It is now a soft springy bounce
On a dry surface all the way
Tossing up and down with every step.
Unlike the walk on the murky surface,
It is a bounce, a dirty bounce.

The dead termite

Its sprawled membrane like wings
Showed vigor prior to its death
A tiring commitment it so clung to
Sticking to it like glue that holds the bones
Until breathlessly and powerlessly it died.

A genuine unadulterated death that needs rewarding;
The gods of nature were awake
Nourished it and cooled its body in the vigor
Evidenced by the shiny globules settling on its wings
As it rested on the cold mornings ground.

Black ants had smelled its dead body
Scent stalking its sweet departure after accomplishment.
In their greed they showed mad disunity
As they pulled it in different directions
Like two bulldozers in a tussle.

The sun rose high and was setting
It illuminated the black ants' fate
Sprawling around the termite in their dry death
With the pungent smell of unripe departure
The pairs lay dead emanating two smells.

Human guise

We show a big smile
When our real feelings are vile
Like the calmness of a salty lake
Misleading a friend to claim it a prank
Showing appearance of peace
Like a newly hatched chick
And nay, inside a big inferno burns in heart.
We tell our daughters the value of being chaste
Yet our eyes shine and burn with lust
The harmlessness of buried coal smoking lightly.
Spreading a net on a path
As if humbly hunting for a buck
Then saying how safe it is trotting the path.
We advice our friends on matters
And then eagerly wait for the backlash
Publicly displaying our clean morality
Moments later, the dents begin showing
What shows but human guile?

Eulogy for a new born

You have sprung forth undefiled
Into the corrupt world
Child; remain listless to its mores.

You will walk a straight path,
You eyes fixed right a head
Turn them not to fields
That you didn't scatter a seed.
Keep your laming feet on track,
And watch over your mind always.

Keep to your tune of infancy
And join not the festering song.
I know you can keep your innocent tune
And infect others with it.

You will be great child,
You are great. Let not
Your hand be dexterous
For what doesn't belong to you
Remain intact child,
And guard yourself against greed
Contract not that disease from others.

Child, welcome to the world!

Struggle of the clock

That clock on top of the monument
Bore a lot of pain in its last breath
As it relentlessly struggled in a stagger
To faithfully complete its course.

In a drunken painful tussle
Like a drunkard pushing his way home
It ticked in almost a mark time movement
Losing sense of time, misleading the passersby.

Slowly it traced its path, taking decades
Like a wounded Oryx almost out of breath
And finally came to its end, 12 O'clock, Zero
It mark timed till it dropped dead.

The clock now rests peacefully
On top of the monument
Dead for decades, still misleading the passersby
It won't soon be repaired and revived
For the monument is timeless anyway.

Prophecy

Standing by the sea shore,
The prophecy came in clear images
Riding on the violent waves of the sea
It came with the image of the future
Built on the present tribal mires and factions.

The images came drifting to the shore
Crude weapons tightly clung in their hands
Tired people weathered by the political impunity
Yet thirsting for the other fellows deficient blood
They came fighting on the waves of the ocean.

The sea water foamed in red
Spraying the bloody water to the shore
A voice called from the middle of the ocean
A muffled voice, choking with bloody water
It called for destruction of this long lived culture.

It drifted across the shore
Went beyond to the land
There where poverty and peril lies
Where ashes of tribal hatred lies
It pleaded for the saving of the sea
Far across the troubled land it faded.

When the night falls

When the night falls
Many walk into the despair of their homes
To share the meager slice the day yielded
And retire in temporarily quenched hunger
Into the unfitting bedding stored in a heap.

When the night falls
Many walk into despondency that engulf them
Visiting them in the invisibility of darkness
Welling sorrow in their disturbed hearts
The sorrow overflows through the eye in tear drops.

When the night falls
Many walk into black markets
Turning into tycoons and rich men overnight
Hoping all will seem to all the daily toil.
Keeping their reputation and image un-tattered.

When the night falls
We worry for the mess we have to pass through
We smile in excitement and expectation we hope for
We weep in the bitter memories of the past
Oh, when the night comes, the spontaneity also comes.

Elegy for Zilpah

Eyes glazed
Hundreds of eyes,
Resting on her lifeless body.
Her body got blurred in the eyes
Tears involuntarily welling in them
Then cascading down the cheeks.

Suppressed cries echoed
A long the morning corridor
They rose, the cries-
Suddenly they were wails
Loudly running out of control.
Weeping flooded the corridor
She remained there
As if in calm sleep.

Hopeful hands touched her chest
Searching for the heartbeat;
All was in vain.
Down the corridor
Patients gathered
Towing the drip suspensions with them

Murmurs left their mouths:-
'How can a medic die?
She gave me my daily dose a while ago . . .'
No words were returned
Only gloomy stares.

Nobody saw the sun that day
All talking of Zilpah
'How could she die?'
Souls silently waited
For her to rise from the sleep
But she had slept for good.
When wheeled away
Renewed weeping arose
"How had she died?"

The last rite

When a guitarist plays a guitar for the last time
He may not know it is his last.
When a weaver fastens the last chord onto a rope
Then weave it then tighten the end knot
Then the last rite is performed,
When he will never weave another rope in his life.

A thought escaping from the mind forever
Like an eagle getting killed far away from its nest
Meets its last rite thus.
The splendor and glamour of tyranny
Faces the best last rite with awakened heathen
Pushing dictators into in-ascendable abyss

The slaves of dictated states walk to freedom
With joined weary hands
Shouting, chanting and voicing their dissatisfaction
Then performing their last rite in unison.